RICHARD WRIGHT

BLACK BOY

Originally edited by Aage Salling and Erik Hvid
Revised by Robert Dewsnap, 1991
Illustrations by Oskar Jørgensen and Gunnar Breiding

EASY READERS
ER
EASY READERS

The vocabulary is based on
Michael West: A General Service List of
English Words, revised & enlarged edition, 1953
Pacemaker Core Vocabulary, 1975
Salling/Hvid: English-Danish Basic Dictionary, 1970
J. A. van Ek: The Threshold Level for Modern Language
Learning in Schools, 1976

Series editor: Ulla Malmmose

Cover layout: Mette Plesner
Cover illustration: Lilian Brøgger

ISBN Denmark 87-23-90099-7
www.easyreader.dk

Easy Readers EGMONT

Printed in Denmark by
Sangill Grafisk Produktion, Holme-Olstrup

RICHARD WRIGHT
(1908-1960)

is one of the great American storytellers of our time. He was born in Mississippi, where his father was a mill and farm worker. When the father left his family and the mother fell ill, the boy was sent to live with relatives. He went to school in Jackson, where his aunt taught. After he left school he worked at several jobs and moved northward to Chicago, where he became a clerk in a post office. He started writing early in his life and traveled widely in Mexico, the Gold Coast (later Ghana), and Europe, where he spent his last years in Paris. From 1932 to 1944 he was a member of the Communist Party. When he left the party, he wrote of his disillusionment, together with five other writers, in The God That Failed.

Black Boy was first published in 1945.

OTHER BOOKS BY RICHARD WRIGHT

Uncle Tom's Children (1938), Native Son (1940), The God That Failed (with others, 1950), The Outsider (1953), Savage Holiday (1954), Black Power (1954), White Man, Listen! (1957), The Long Dream (1958), Eight Men (1961), Lawd Today (1963).

MICHIGAN
DETROIT
CHICAGO
ILLINOIS
TENNESSEE
ARKANSAS
MEMPHIS
MISSISSIPPI
ALABAMA
JACKSON
NATCHEZ
MOBILE
GULF OF MEXICO
ATLANTIC OCEAN
N
W
E
S
UNITED STATES
200miles
200km

1

It was a winter morning long ago. I was four years old. I found myself standing before a *fireplace*, warming my hands over the fire, listening to the wind. All morning, my mother had been telling me that I must make no noise. And I was angry. In the next room, *Granny* lay ill, under the care of a doctor night and day. I knew that I would be beaten if I did not keep quiet. I crossed to the window. I pushed back the *curtains* – which I was not allowed to touch – and looked into the street. I was dreaming of running and playing and shouting, but the thought of Granny's old white face made me afraid.

The house was quiet. My brother – a year younger than I – was playing upon the floor. A bird flew past the window and I shouted.

"You had better keep quiet," my brother said.

"You *shut up*," I said.

My mother came into the room and closed the door behind her. She came to me and shook her finger in my face.

"You stop that shouting, you hear!" she said. "You know that Granny is ill, and you had better keep quiet." Then she left the room.

"I told you so," my brother said.

"You shut up," I told him again.

I walked about the room, trying to think of something to do. There was nothing of interest except

---

fireplace: see picture, page 6
Granny, Grandmother
curtains: see picture, page 6
shut up, shut your mouth

the fire, and *finally* I stood before it, looking at the red *flames.*

An idea of a new kind of game came into my mind. Why not throw something into the fire and watch it burn? There was only my picture-book. My mother

finally, in the end

would beat me if I burnt that. Then what? The *broom*!

I tore a few *straws* out of the broom and threw them into the fire and watched them burn. Who would care about that? Burning straws was a good game, and I took more of them from the broom and threw them into the fire. My brother came to my side.

"Don't do that," he said.

"Why?" I asked.

"You'll burn the whole broom," he said.

"You shut up," I said.

"I'll tell Mother," he said.

"And I'll beat you," I said.

A new thought came to me. What would the long white curtains look like if I lit some straws and held them under the curtains? Would I try it? Yes. I pulled some straws from the broom and held them to the fire. I ran to the window and brought the flame to the curtains. My brother shook his head.

"No," he said.

He spoke too lake. The flames were eating the curtains. I stepped back. The fire climbed quickly up to the top of the window. I was afraid and looked round for my brother; he was gone. The room was full of smoke and flames. I ran to the kitchen; there was smoke there too. Soon my mother would see the fire and beat me. I had done something wrong, yes. I would run away and never come back. I ran out of the kitchen. Where could I go? Yes, under the house!

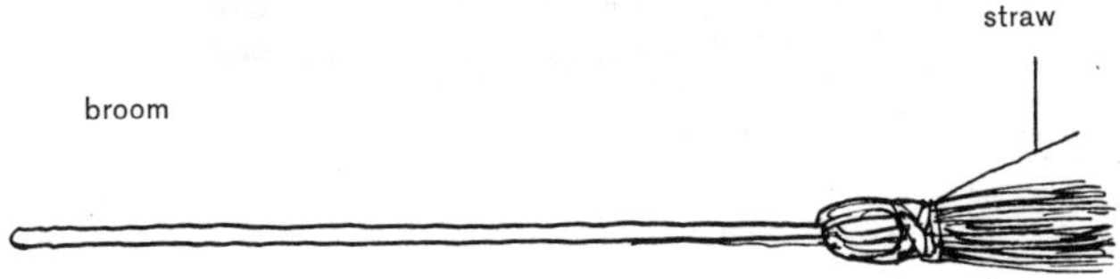

Nobody would find me there. I crept under the house, so that nobody would find me and beat me.

Soon I heard footsteps on the floor above me. Then I heard shouts. Later, the sound of the *fire engines* came from the street. Yes, there really was a fire. Once before, I had seen a house burn down. I was afraid. I thought of my grandmother lying on her bed with yellow flames in her black hair. Would my mother burn? Would my brother burn? Perhaps everybody in the house would burn! Why had I not thought of that before I set fire to the curtains?

"Richard!" my mother called.

I saw her legs moving outside the house. Her face came down to the ground. She had found me! Her face went away; no, she had not seen me.

"Richard! The house is on fire. Oh, find my child!"

Yes, the house was on fire, but I had decided not to come out. Then I saw another face looking under the house; it was my father's. "There he is!" he cried.

"No!" I *screamed.*

"Come here, boy!"

"No!"

fire engine

---

scream, shout in fear, in a loud, high voice

"The house is on fire!"

"Leave me alone!"

He crept in to me and took hold of one of my legs.

"Come out of there, you little fool!"

"Let me go!"

He pulled me out. It was over. I would be beaten. I did not care any more. I knew what was coming. The moment his hand left me, I jumped up and ran. I was caught before I had run ten steps.

I do not remember much of what happened after that, except that no one had died in the fire and half of the house still stood. The men of the family had carried Granny out of the house. But I was beaten so long and so hard that they had to call a doctor. He said that I must stay in bed, in a quiet room, if they wanted me to live. I was ill in bed for a long time. And afterwards, I knew that my mother had come close to killing me.

* * *

One day, my mother told me that we were going to Memphis, on a boat called the Kate Adams. I could hardly wait to go, and the days seemed to have no end. Each night I went to bed hoping that the next morning would be the great day.

"How big is the boat?" I asked my mother.

"As big as a mountain," she said.

"Has it got a *whistle*?"

"Yes."

"Does the whistle blow?"

"Yes."

"When?"

"When the captain wants it to blow."

---

whistle: see picture, page 10

"Why do they call it the Kate Adams?"
"Because that is the boat's name."
"What color is the boat?"
"White."
"How long will we be on the boat?"
"All day and night."
"Will we sleep on the boat?"
"Yes, we'll sleep. Now, be quiet!"

For days I had dreamed about a big white boat sailing on the water. Then my mother took me down on the day we were leaving and I saw a small, dirty boat that was not at all like the boat of my dreams. When the time came to go on board the boat, I cried. My mother thought that I did not want to go with her to Memphis; and I could not tell her what was the matter. But I felt better when I walked about the boat and looked at the *Negroes* eating, talking, and singing. I was happy when my father took me down into the engine room, and I stayed there for hours.

Negro, black person

In Memphis we lived in a big old house. For all the four of us, we had only a kitchen and a bedroom. There was space for us to play outside the house, but for days I was afraid to go into the strange city streets alone. And I missed the green, growing things of our old garden.

My father worked at night in a *store*. He slept in the daytime, so we had to be quiet. He was the lawgiver in our family, and I never laughed when he was present.

One morning my brother and I found a *kitten* that started a loud meowing. We gave it some food and water, but it still meowed. My father came to the back door and told us to be quiet. We told him it was the kitten that was making the noise. He ordered us to drive it away. We tried to make the kitten leave, but it would not move.

"Go away!" my father shouted.

The kitten just meowed.

"Kill the thing!" my father shouted. "Do something, get it away from here!"

He went inside. I did not like his shouting. What could I do to hit back at him? Oh, yes ... He had told us to kill the kitten and I would kill it. I knew that he did not really mean me to kill the kitten. But I decided to do exactly as he had said.

"He told us to kill the kitten," I said to my brother.

"He didn't mean it," my brother said.

"He did, and you heard him."

My brother ran away. I found a piece of *rope*, and put it round the kitten's neck. Then, I took the rope

---

store, shop
kitten, rope: see picture, page 12

over a *nail*, and pulled the kitten's feet off the ground. It opened its mouth, and its *tongue* shot out. I went to find my brother.

"I killed it," I said.

"You did bad," my brother said.

"Now Papa can sleep," I said.

"He didn't mean you to kill it," my brother said.

"Then why did he tell me to do it?" I asked.

My brother could not answer; he looked at the kitten hanging down from the nail.

"I'm going to tell," my brother said, running into the house.

I waited. My mother came up to me. She stopped when she saw the kitten hanging from the rope.

"What have you done?" she asked.

"The kitten was making a noise and Papa told me to kill it," I answered.

"You little fool!" she said. "Your father is going to beat you for this."

"But he told me to kill it."

"You shut your mouth."

She took me to my father's bedside and told him what I had done.

"You know better than that!" my father shouted.

"You told me to kill it," I said.

"I told you to drive it away," he said.

"You told me to kill it."

"You get out before I hit you," my father shouted, and turned over in bed.

I was happy, because now I had told my father that I didn't like him. He now knew one thing: if he beat me, I would never believe his words again.

But my mother knew what to do. She waited until it was time for me to go to bed. Then she ordered me to go out into the dark and *bury* the kitten.

"No!" I screamed. I was afraid to go out alone.

"Get out of here and bury the kitten," she ordered.

"I'm afraid!"

"And wasn't the kitten afraid when you put that rope round its neck?" she asked.

"But it was only a kitten," I said.

"But it was alive," she said. "Can you make it live again?"

"But Papa told me to kill it," I said.

My mother hit me on the mouth. "You stop that lying! You know what he meant! Go out there and dig a hole and bury that kitten!"

I went out into the black night. Though I knew that

---

bury, put in a hole in the ground

I had killed the kitten, my mother's words had made it live again in my mind. What would that kitten do to me if I touched it?

"Mother, come and stand by me," I *begged* her.

"You didn't stand by that kitten, so why should I stand by you?" she asked.

"I can't touch it," I said, crying.

"Take it down!" she ordered.

I took the rope off the nail. The kitten fell down, with a sound that stayed in my ears for many days and nights. Then I buried the kitten and went back to the house. But my mother took my hand and led me to the kitten's *grave* again.

"Shut your eyes and say after me," she said.

I closed my eyes, holding her hand.

"Dear God, our Father, I am sorry for what I have done: *forgive me*, for I knew not what I was doing ..."

"Dear God, our Father, I am sorry for what I have done: forgive me, for I knew not what I was doing," I said.

* * *

At first I did not really know what *hunger* meant. Now, I began to wake up at night to find hunger standing at my bedside, looking at me with wide open eyes. I had known hunger before this, but that had been a normal hunger. It had made me ask for food. This new hunger made me angry. When I asked for food, my mother would now give me a cup of tea.

---

beg, ask with deep feeling
grave, hole in the ground where he had buried the kitten
forgive me, accept the fact that I am sorry
hunger, feeling of being hungry

This would help for a moment or two, but a little later I would feel hunger again. I did not play as much as before. For the first time in my life, I had to stop and think of what was happening to me.

"Oh, Mama, I'm hungry," I said one afternoon.

"Jump up and catch a kungry," she said, trying to make me laugh and forget.

"What's a kungry?"

"It's what little boys eat when they get hungry," she said.

"What does it taste like?"

"I don't know."

"Then why do you tell me to catch one?"

"Because you said you were hungry," she said, smiling.

But this made me angry.

"I'm hungry. I want to eat."

"You'll have to wait."

"But I want to eat now."

"But there's nothing to eat," she told me.

"Why?"

"Just because there's none."

"But I want to eat," I said, beginning to cry.

"You'll have to wait," she said again.

"But why?"

"For God to send some food."

"When is He going to send it?"

"I don't know."

"But I'm hungry."

She looked at me with tears in her eyes.

"Where's your father?" she asked me.

I looked at her. Yes, it was true: my father had not come home to sleep for many days now. I could make as much noise as I wanted. But I had not understood what this meant: there would be no food.

"I don't know," I said.

"Who brings food into the house?" my mother asked me.

"Papa," I said. "He always brought food."

"Well, your father isn't here now," she said.

"Where is he?"

"I don't know," she said.

"But I'm hungry," I said.

"You'll have to wait until I find work and buy food," she said.

My mother at last went to work as a cook. She then left me and my brother alone in the house each day with a *loaf of bread* and a *pot of tea.*

loaf of bread

teapot

When she came back in the evening, she would be tired and would cry a lot. Sometimes she would call us to her and talk to us for hours. She would tell us that we now had no father, and that we must learn to take care of ourselves. We did not understand what had happened between our father and our mother. Sometimes we asked her why father had left. She would then tell us that we were too young to know.

One evening, my mother told me that I would have to do the shopping for food. She took me to the store at the corner of the street, to show me the way. I felt pleased with myself. The next afternoon, I took the *basket* and went down the street towards the store. When I got to the corner, a group of boys knocked me down. As I fell, they took my basket and the money, and sent me running home in fear. That evening, I told my mother what had happened. She said nothing. She sat down at once, wrote another note, gave me more money, and sent me out to the store again. I walked down the steps and saw the same boys playing in the street. I ran back into the house.

"What's the matter?" my mother asked.

"It's those same boys," I said. "They'll beat me."

"You've got to get over that," she said. "Now, go on."

"I'm afraid," I said.

"Go on," she said. "Now, go on."

I went out of the door and walked quickly down the street.

"There he is!" someone cried.

They came towards me and I broke into a wild run towards home. They knocked me down again. They took the money out of my hand, gave me a few *slaps*, and sent me home crying. My mother met me at the door.

"They beat me," I said. "They took the money."

"Don't you come in here," my mother said.

"But they're coming after me."

basket

---

slap, a blow with the open hand

"You just stay where you are," she said. "I'm going to teach you this night to stand up and fight for yourself."

She went into the house and I waited. Then she came out with more money and another note; she also had a long heavy stick.

"Take this money, this note, and this stick," she said. "Go to the store, and if these boys do anything to you, then fight."

"But I'm afraid," I said.

"Don't you come into this house until you've got the things from the store," she said.

"They'll beat me; they'll beat me," I said.

"Then stay in the streets; don't come back here!"

I ran up the steps and tried to get past her into the house. A hard slap came on my face. I stood in the street, crying.

"Please let me wait till tomorrow," I said.

"No," she said. "Go now! If you come back into the house, I'll beat you."

She shut the door. I was alone in the dark street. It was clear to me: I was going to be beaten either in the street or at home. I tried to think. If I were beaten at home, there was nothing I could do about it; but if I were beaten in the streets, I at least had a chance to fight. I took the stick and walked down the street.

"There he is again!" the cry went up.

They came up to me and tried to take the money from my hand.

"I'll kill you!" I cried.

They came nearer. I let the stick fly and heard it hit a boy's head. I struck again, hitting another boy. I fought to knock them down, to kill them. I hit again

and again. The boys moved away; they had never seen anyone so angry. I stood still and asked them to come on and fight. They didn't, and I ran after them. They ran home, crying, and their fathers came into the street. For the first time in my life, I shouted at grown-ups. I told them that I would give them the same if they touched me. Then I went to the store. On my way back, I held the stick in my hand, ready for use, but there was not a boy to be seen. That night I won the right to the streets of Memphis.

* * *

One summer afternoon – in my sixth year – I was looking under the doors of a *saloon.* A black man caught hold of my arm and pulled me into the room. I cried and tried to break free of him, afraid of the crowd of men and women, but he would not let me

---

saloon: see picture, page 20

In the saloon

go. He sat me on the *counter*, put his hat upon my head, and ordered a drink for me. The crowd shouted with pleasure. Somebody tried to put a cigar in my mouth, but I turned my head away.

"How do you feel, sitting there like a man, boy?" a man asked.

"Make him *drunk* and he'll stop looking in here," somebody said.

"Let's buy him drinks," another said.

Some of my fear left me, as I looked at the people. A drink of whisky was set before me.

---

drunk, full of alcoholic drink

"Drink it, boy," somebody said.

I shook my head. The man who had pulled me into the saloon put the glass to my mouth. I said no.

"Drink it, you'll feel good," he said.

I drank. The men and women laughed. The crowd came up to stand around me, asking me to drink. I drank again. My head began to turn around and I laughed. I drank again and again, and I ran laughing and shouting among the crowd. As I would pass each man, I would drink out of his glass. Soon I was drunk.

A man called me to him and whispered some words quietly in my ear. He told me to go and say the words to a woman. Then, he said, he would give me a *nickel.* I told him that I would say the words. He gave me the nickel, and I ran to the woman and shouted the words. A storm of laughter went up in the saloon.

"Don't teach the boy that," someone said.

"He doesn't know what it is," another said.

From then on, for a *penny* or a nickel, I would say to anyone whatever was whispered to me. I ran from person to person, shouting things that made them roll with laughter.

"Let the boy alone now," someone said.

"It won't hurt him," another said.

"Go home, boy," somebody shouted at me.

They let me go. I walked along the street, drunk, shouting the things I had learnt in the saloon.

a nickel: 5 cents

a penny: 1 cent

After that, many an evening my mother would find me in the streets, drunk. She would take me home and beat me. But the next morning, when she had gone to work, I would run to the saloon. There I would wait for someone to take me in and buy me a drink.

My mother talked to the man who owned the saloon. He told me not to come in, but the men would buy me drinks anyway.

I was a *drunkard* in my sixth year, before I had begun school. I wandered through the streets with a *gang* of children, begging for money. I saw more than I could understand and heard more than I could remember. My mother did not know what to do. She beat me and cried over me, telling me that she had to work. Finally she sent me and my brother to an old black woman. This woman watched me every moment to keep me from running to the doors of the saloons to beg for whisky. Finally I lost my desire for alcohol and I forgot the taste of it.

In the afternoon the schoolchildren would stop outside the house and play. They would leave their books on the ground. I would turn the pages of the books and ask the children what was in them. Then I began to learn some of the words. I told my mother that I wanted to learn to read, and she helped me. Soon I was able to read slowly through most of the children's books.

This made me want to know about things. When

---

drunkard, a person who is often drunk
gang, group of people who go around together or who work together

my mother came home from a hard day's work, I would ask her everything about what I had heard in the streets. I would ask her so many questions that she told me she could not talk to me any more.

* * *

One cold morning, my mother called me. She told me that there was no coal in the house, so we could make no fire. She was taking my brother with her to work, and I must stay in bed. Then the man would come with the coal, she said. I went back to sleep, and woke up when somebody rang the bell. I opened the door, and let in the coal-man.

"Are you cold?" he asked.

"Yes," I said.

When I had given him money he said, "How much money should I give you back?"

"I don't know," I said.

"Don't you know how to count?"

"No, sir," I said.

"Listen and say after me," he said.

He counted to ten and I listened. Then he asked me to count alone and I did. He then taught me the words twenty, thirty, forty, etc. Then he told me to add one, two, three, and so on. In about half an hour's time I had learnt to count to a hundred. I was very happy. Long after the coal-man had gone, I danced up and down on the bed, counting again and again to a hundred. I was afraid that I would forget how to do it. When my mother came back, I told her to stand still and listen to me while I counted to one hundred. She was too surprised to speak.

I began school at a later age than was usual; my mother had not been able to buy me the clothes to make me look like the other children. The boys of the street took me to school the first day. When we arrived there, I was afraid, and wanted to return home. But the boys took my hand and pulled me inside the building. I was still afraid, and the other children had to tell the teacher my name and address. I sat listening to the other children. They spoke when the teacher asked them to, but I could not open my mouth.

In the playground I found myself in a group of older boys and followed them about, listening to their talk. In half an hour I learned more about men and women, boys and girls than anybody had ever told me before, and not in the best language. When I came home, my head was full of new things, but not a single idea from books. I ate my food quickly, took a piece of soap and ran into the street. I wanted to show people all I had learned in school since morning.

I went from window to window and wrote in big soap-letters all the words the boys had told me. I had written on nearly all the windows in the street when a woman stopped me and drove me home. That night the woman came to see my mother and told her what I had done. She took my mother from window to window, to show her my writings. My mother wanted to know where I had learned those words. I said I had learned them at school, but she did not believe me. My mother got a *pail* of water and a piece of cloth, took me by the hand, and led me to the first window.

"Now, wash until that word is gone," she ordered.

People stood around me. They asked my mother

---

pail: see picture, page 26

how I could have learned so much so quickly. I washed windows until I grew blind with *anger.* I cried and begged Mother to let me go. I told her that I would never write such words again. She did not let me go until the last soap-word had been washed away. Never again did I write words like that; I kept them to myself.

* * *

My mother fell ill and food became a problem.

---

anger, the feeling of being angry

Hunger was with us always. Sometimes the *neighbors* would feed us, or a dollar would come from my grandmother. It was winter, and I would go out every morning to buy a paper bag full of coal. For a time, I stayed away from school to look after my mother, then Granny came to visit us and I returned to school.

At night there was much talk about our going to live with Granny, but nothing came of it. Granny went home and left us a few dollars. Finally we could not pay for the rooms we lived in. My mother went out to find a place where she could send us. She found an *orphan* home, and one morning my mother took me and my brother to the place.

The house was full of children and there was always a storm of noise. The meals were small, and there were only two of them. If a child did anything bad he was sent to bed without food.

At the beginning my mother came to see us every night. Then her visits stopped. I began to wonder if she, like my father, had gone away never to come back. So when she did come, I asked her why she had stayed away so long. She told me what the people at the orphan home had said to her: that it was not good for us if she came too often. I begged my mother to take me away; she cried and told me that soon she would take us to Arkansas.

I decided that as soon as night came I would run away. When dinner came, I did not go to the table, but hid behind a door. When I heard the others eating, I opened the door and ran down the street. Dark was

---

neighbor, person living in one of the nearest houses (in British English: *neighbour)*
orphan, child that has lost its father and mother

coming and I was afraid. People passed me. Where was I going? I did not know. No, I could not go on. I would go back. But I had walked so far and turned so many corners. Which way led back? I did not know. I was lost.

I stood in the middle of the street and cried. A "white" policeman came up to me and asked me what was the matter. I told him that I was trying to find my mother. A crowd gathered and I was asked where I lived. I was too full of fear to cry now. I wanted to tell the "white" policeman that I had run off from an orphan home and that Miss Simon was the head of it, but I was afraid. Finally I was taken to the police station, where they gave me something to eat. I felt better. Through the window I could see that it was dark. I fell asleep. When I opened my eyes, another policeman was sitting beside me. Before I knew it, I had told him that I had run away from an orphan home and that Miss Simon was the head of it.

A few minutes later I was walking beside a policeman towards the home. The policeman led me to the house, and I saw Miss Simon standing on the steps waiting for me. When the policeman had left, I begged her not to beat me. But she took me to an empty room and beat me long and hard. In bed that night I decided to run away again, but they watched me closely.

My mother was told about it and she was afraid. "Why did you do it?" she asked.

"I don't want to stay here," I said.

"But you must," she said. "You must remember that you have no father. I'm doing all I can."

"I don't want to stay here," I said.

2

My mother arrived at the orphan home one afternoon with the news that we were going to live with her sister in Elaine, Arkansas. On the way there, we would visit Granny in Jackson, Mississippi. I was very happy and ran about to gather my clothes.

I could hardly wait to leave, and stood in the hall ready to go. I did not even think of saying goodbye to the boys and girls with whom I had eaten and slept and lived for so many weeks. My mother told me to shake hands with them, and I did. In later years, I often had to do things which other people expected of me. I did these things although I did not and could not feel what the other people felt.

In Granny's house lived a *colored* schoolteacher, Ella. She was a young woman whom I liked very much though I was afraid of her. She was always reading books. I had long wanted to ask her to tell me about the books, but I dared not. One afternoon I found her alone in the garden, reading.

"Ella," I said, "please tell me what you are reading."

"It's just a book," she said.

"But what's it about?" I asked.

"Your grandmother wouldn't like it if I talked to you about books," she told me.

"I don't care," I said.

"Shh – you mustn't say things like that."

"But I want to know."

---

colored, (of a person), not white (in British English: *coloured)*

"When you grow up, you'll read books and know what's in them," she explained.

"But I want to know now."

She thought a while, then closed the book.

"Come here," she said.

I sat at her feet and looked up at her.

"Once upon a time there was an old, old man named Bluebeard," she began in a low voice.

She whispered to me the story of Bluebeard and His Seven Wives, and I no longer saw the garden, the sunshine, her face, or anything else. As her words fell upon my ears, they became real in a way I had never known before. She told me how Bluebeard had married his seven wives, how he had loved and killed them, how he had hanged them up by their hair in a dark room. The story made the world around me be, live, move; the look of things changed and the world became different. I stopped her all the time to ask her questions. The feelings the story called up in me were never to leave me. When Ella was about to finish, Granny came out.

"You stop that, you bad girl!" she shouted. "I want none of that in my house."

For a moment I did not know what was happening.

"I'm sorry, Mrs Wilson," Ella said. "But he asked me -"

"He's just a child and you know it," Granny said angrily.

Ella bowed her head and went into the house.

* * *

We were at the railroad station with our bags, waiting for the train that would take us to Arkansas. For the first time, I saw there were two lines of people at the *ticket window*, a "white" line and a "black" line. When we were on the train, I found that we Negroes were in one part of the train and that the whites were in another.

"Can I go and look at the white *folks*?" I asked my mother.

"You keep quiet," she said.

"But that wouldn't be wrong, would it?"

"Will you keep still!"

"But why can't I?"

I had begun to notice that my mother became angry when I asked her questions about whites and blacks. I could not quite understand her. I wanted to understand one thing: why did those two sets of people, who lived side by side, never touch unless they fought? Now, there was my grandmother ... Was she white? Just how white was she? What did the whites think of her whiteness?

"Mama, is Granny white?" I asked as the train rolled through the darkness.

"If you've got eyes, you can see what color she is," my mother said.

"I mean, do the white folks think she's white?"

"Why don't you ask the white folks that?"

"But you know."

"Why should I know?" she asked. "I'm not white."

"Granny looks white," I said. "Then why does she live with us colored folks?"

---

ticket window: see picture, page 32
folks, people

"Don't you want Granny to live with us?" she asked.

"Yes."

"Then why are you asking?"

"I want to know."

"Doesn't Granny live with us?"

"Yes."

"Isn't that enough?"

"But does she want to live with us?"

"Why didn't you ask Granny that?"

"Did Granny become colored when she married Grandpa?"

"Will you stop asking silly questions!"

"But did she?"

"Granny didn't **become** colored," my mother said angrily. "She was **born** the color she is now."

"Why didn't Granny marry a white man?" I asked.

"Because she didn't want to."

"Why don't you want to talk to me?" I asked.

She slapped me, and I cried. Later, she explained that Granny's parents and grandparents had been Irish, Scotch and French, and Negro.

"What was Granny's name before she married Grandpa?"

"Her name was Bolden."

"Who gave her that name?"

"The white man who owned her."

"She was a *slave*?"

"Yes."

"And Bolden was the name of Granny's father?"

"Granny doesn't know who her father was."

"So they just gave her any name?"

"They gave her a name; that's all I know."

---

slave, person who is forced to work for no money

"Couldn't Granny find out who her father was?"

"For what, silly?"

"So she could know."

"Know for what?"

"Just to know."

"But for what?"

I could not say. I could not get anywhere.

"Mama, where did Father get his name?"

"From his father."

"And where did the father of my father get his name?"

"Like Granny got hers. From a white man."

"Do they know who he is?"

"I don't know."

"Why don't they find out?"

"For what?" my mother asked.

And I could think of no reason why my father should try to find out who his father's father was.

"What has Papa got in him?" I asked.

"Some white and some red and some black," she said.

"Indian, white, and Negro?"

"Yes."

"Then what am I?"

"They'll call you a colored man when you grow up," she said. Then she turned to me, smiled and said: "Do you mind, Mr Wright?"

I was angry and I did not answer.

* * *

When we arrived in Elaine, I saw that Aunt Maggie lived in a house with a *fence* around it. It looked like home and I was glad. Aunt Maggie's husband, Uncle

Hoskins, owned a saloon. I asked him several times to take me to see it and he promised; but my mother said no. Well, if I could not see the saloon, I could at least eat. And there was so much food on Aunt Maggie's table that I could not believe it was real. It took me some time to get used to the idea that there was enough to eat. I felt that if I ate enough there would not be anything left for another time. When I first sat down at Aunt Maggie's table, I could not eat until I had asked:

"Can I eat all I want?"

"Eat as much as you like," said Uncle Hoskins.

I did not believe him. I ate until my *stomach* hurt,

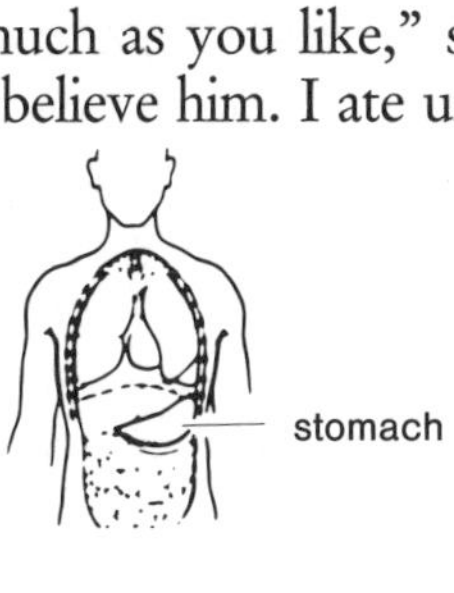

and even then I did not get up from the table.

"Your eyes are bigger than your stomach," my mother said.

"Let him eat all he wants to and get used to food," Uncle Hoskins said.

When the evening meal was over, I saw that there was a lot of bread left on the table. I was afraid that there would be no bread for breakfast in the morning. So I took some pieces of bread and hid them about the house, in corners and under my bed, until I was sure that there would always be bread in the morning.

Every day Uncle Hoskins went to his saloon in the evening and did not return home until the early hours of the morning. Like my father, he slept in the daytime. My brother and I shouted and made as much noise as we liked, and he did not seem to care. Often I went into his room while he slept and stared at the big revolver that lay near his head. I asked Aunt Maggie why he kept the gun so close to him. She told me that some men had said they would kill him, white men ...

One morning I woke up to learn that Uncle Hoskins had not come home from the saloon. Aunt Maggie wanted to go to the saloon to see what had happened; but Uncle Hoskins had told her never to go there. The day passed and dinner-time came.

"I'm going to find out if anything has happened," Aunt Maggie said. But she did not go. It grew dark, and still he had not come.

"I hope the white people didn't do anything to him," she said.

Later she went into the bedroom, and when she came out she said:

"He didn't take his gun. I wonder what could have happened?"

We ate without a word being said. An hour later there was the sound of footsteps outside. Aunt Maggie ran to the door. A tall black boy stood there. He took off his hat.

"Mr Hoskins ... he's been shot. Been shot by a white man," the boy said. "Mrs Hoskins, he's dead."

Aunt Maggie cried out, and ran into the street.

"Don't you go to the saloon," the boy called. "They'll kill you if you go there. White folks say they'll kill all his family."

My mother pulled Aunt Maggie back into the house. That night, we put all our clothes and things in a farmer's *wagon*, and before morning we were rolling away. We got rooms at West Helena, and Aunt Maggie and my mother kept inside the house all day. They were afraid to be seen on the streets. But at night Aunt Maggie went back to Elaine several times, and she would tell no one except my mother when she was going.

My mother and Aunt Maggie cooked in the houses of white folks, and my brother and I were free to play

wagon

where we wanted all day. I lived in West Helena a long time before I returned to school. My mother got a job in a doctor's house at very good pay, five dollars a week. At once she told everyone that her "sons were going to school again". I was happy, but I was still afraid. On the first day at school, the whole class laughed at me. I had to go to the *blackboard* to write my name and address. I knew my name and address, knew how to write it, knew how to spell it. But then, standing at the blackboard with the eyes of the many girls and boys looking at my back made me go cold inside, and I could not write a single letter.

"Write your name," the teacher called to me.

I took up the white *chalk* and I was about to write when my mind went *blank*. I could not remember my name, not even the first letter. Someone began to laugh quietly.

"Just forget us and write your name and address," the teacher said.

My hand could not move.

"Don't you know your name?" the teacher asked.

I looked at her and could not answer. The teacher came to my side.

"What's your name?" she asked.

"Richard," I whispered.

"Richard what?"

"Richard Wright," I said.

"*Spell* it."

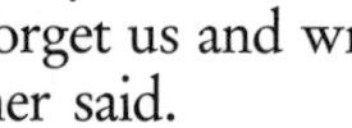
chalk

---

blank, empty
spell, say the letters in the name: R-i-c-h-a-r-d W-r-i-g-h-t

I spelled my name.

"Now write it."

Again I turned to the blackboard and put up my hand, but I could do nothing. The whole room started to laugh. "You may go to your seat," the teacher said.

I knew how to write as well as any boy or girl in the classroom. I could read better than any of them, and I could talk well when I was sure of myself. Then why did strange faces make me go cold and empty?

While sitting in class one day, I was surprised to hear bells ringing. Soon there was a lot of noise. The boys and girls ran to the windows. The teacher left the room. When she came back, she said:

"Everyone can go home."

"Why?"

"The war is over," the teacher said.

I followed the rest of the children into the street and saw that black and white people were laughing and singing and shouting. I felt afraid as I went through crowds of white people; but my fear left me when I came into my own street and saw smiling black faces. I noticed that many boys and girls were looking at something in the sky; I looked up and saw what seemed to be a little bird.

"Look!"

"A *plane*!"

I had never seen a plane.

"It's a bird," I said.

The crowd laughed.

"That's a plane, boy," a man said.

"It's a bird," I said. "I see it."

A man lifted me upon his *shoulder*.

"Boy, remember this," he said. "You're seeing a man fly."

I still did not believe it. It still looked like a bird to me. That night at home, my mother told me that men could fly.

plane
shoulder

3

Having grown taller and older, I now made friends with older boys. In the afternoons, when school was over, I would walk down the street. Then I would see one or more of the gang waiting at a corner, or sitting on somebody's doorstep.

"Hey."

"Have you eaten yet?"

"Yeah, man."

"They say a white man hit a colored man up North, and that the colored man hit the white man, and nobody did a thing."

"Man for man up there."

"They say they have got houses in New York forty *stories* high!"

"Man, I would be afraid of those houses."

"You know, they say that those buildings rock in the wind."

"No, *nigger.*"

"Yeah, they say they do."

"You think that could be?"

"No! If a building rocked in the wind it would fall. Any fool knows that."

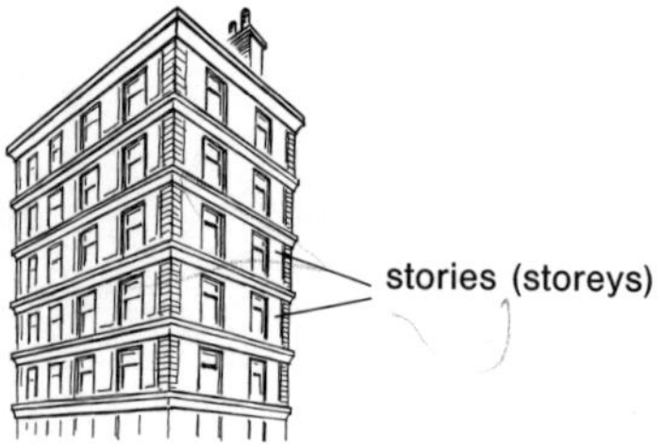

---

nigger, black person

We were now big enough for the white boys to fear us. Now both of us, the white boys and the black boys, began to play our *roles* as white and black. We played these roles as if we had been born to them and they were in our blood. If the white boys came to our side of the railroad, we threw stones at them. If we happened to find ourselves on their side, they threw stones at us.

My mother became too ill to work, and I began to do small jobs near where we lived. My first job was to carry lunches to the men who worked on the railroad, for which they gave me 25 cents a week. When the men did not finish their lunches, I ate what was left over. Later I got a job in a café, carrying wood in my arms to keep the big *stove* going. I got a dollar a week for this work.

One morning a shouting voice woke me.

"Richard! Richard!"

I rolled out of bed. My brother came running into the room.

"Richard! You'd better come and see Mama. She is very ill," he said.

I ran into my mother's room and saw her lying

stove

---

role, part, as in a theater

upon her bed, her eyes open. She was very still.

"Mama!" I called.

She did not answer or turn her head. I went forward to touch her. But I stepped back, afraid that she was dead.

"Mama!" I called again, not able to understand that she could not answer.

My brother and I looked at each other; we did not know what to do.

"We had better get somebody," I said.

I ran into the hall and called a neighbor. A tall, black woman came out of a door.

"Please, won't you come and see my mama? She won't talk. We can't wake her up. She's very ill," I told the woman.

She followed me.

"Mrs Wright!" she called to my mother.

My mother lay still.

"She isn't dead," she said. "But she's ill, all right. I had better get some more of the neighbors."

Five or six women came. My brother and I waited in the hall while they took her clothes off and put her to bed.

When we were allowed back in the room, a woman said:

"Looks like a *stroke* to me."

"And she's so young."

One of the women asked if there was any money in the house. I did not know. They looked around and found a dollar or two and sent for a doctor. The doctor arrived. Yes, he told us, my mother had had a

---

stroke, sudden trouble with the blood supply inside the head

stroke. Someone must be with her day and night, and she must have medicine. Where was her husband? I told him how my father had left us, and he shook his head.

"She'll need all the help she can get," the doctor said. "She cannot talk, and someone will have to help her eat."

I wrote a letter to Granny, asking her to come and help us. The neighbors looked after my mother day and night, gave us food and washed our clothes. What if Grannny did not come? Though I was a child, I could no longer feel as a child. I was glad that my mother was not dead, but she would be ill for a very long time. When Granny came, I left everything to her.

I wrote letters for Granny to her eight children, asking for money with which "to take Ella and her two little children to our home". Money came, and my mother was taken to the train in an *ambulance*.

We rode to Jackson, and my mother was put to bed. Doctors came and went. Night and day I could hear *groans* from her room. We thought that she would die at any moment.

---

groan, deep sound made by someone who is ill

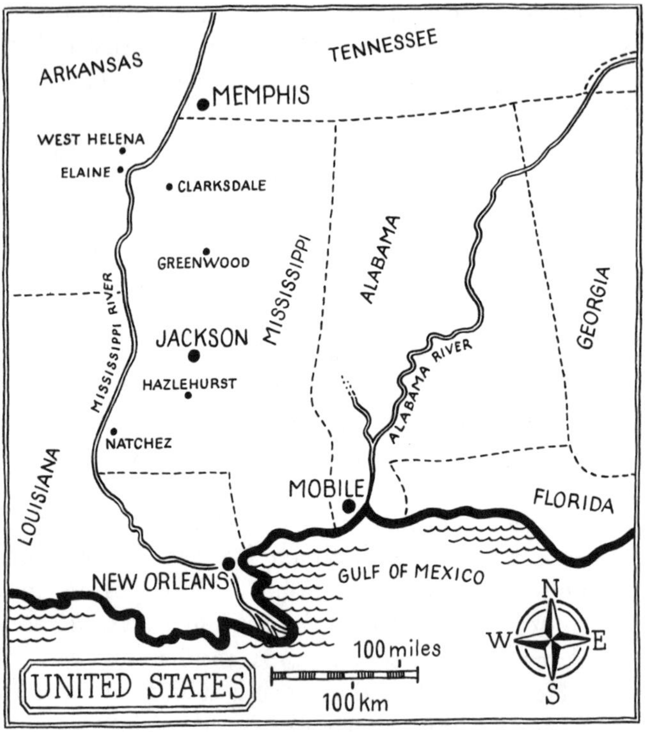

Aunt Maggie, who had left us some time before, came back from Detroit. Aunt Cleo came from Chicago. Uncle Clark came from Greenwood, Mississippi. Uncle Edward came from Carters, Mississippi. Uncle Charles from Mobile, Alabama. Aunt Addie from a religious school in Huntsville, Alabama. Uncle Thomas from Hazlehurst, Mississippi. I heard whispered talk of "what is to become of her children?" I felt afraid. At night my sleep was filled with wild dreams.

One night I found myself standing in the yard. The moon was shining. Suddeny, I felt that someone was holding my hand. I looked and saw one of my uncles. He was speaking to me in a low, gentle voice.

"What's the matter, son?"

I looked at him, trying to understand what he was saying.

"Richard, what are you doing?"

I could not answer. It seemed that I could not wake up. He shook me. I came to myself.

"Where are we going?" I asked him.

"You were walking in your sleep," he said.

One evening my brother and I were called into the front room, where all the uncles and aunts were gathered.

"Richard," said an uncle, "Aunt Maggie is going to take your brother to Detroit and send him to school."

I waited. Who was going to take me?

"Now, where would you like to go?"

"Anywhere," I said.

"Any of us is willing to take you."

Quickly I thought which of them lived nearest to Jackson. Uncle Clark lived in Greenwood, which was only a few miles away.

"I'd like to live with Uncle Clark, since he's close to the home here," I said.

"Is that what you really want?"

"Yes, sir."

"All right. I'll take you back with me and send you to school. Tomorrow we'll go and buy clothes."

* * *

Uncle Clark took me to school. The first half of the day passed well enough. The books were easy, and I felt that I could keep up. But my fear was still in me. Were the boys easy to get on with? How hard did they fight?

At *noon* I went into the playground. A group of boys came up to me and looked at me from head to foot.

"Where are you from?" a boy asked.

"Jackson," I answered.

"Why don't they make people nice to look at in Jackson?" he asked.

"You're not so nice to look at yourself."

"Oh!"

"Oh!"

"You hear what he told him?"

"I don't want to fight," I said. "But if you want to, I'll fight."

"Hard, are you?"

"As hard as you."

The boy came close. He put his face right in front of mine.

"You think I'm afraid of you, don't you?" he asked.

Somebody pushed the boy into me. I pushed him back, hard.

"Don't push me!" the boy said.

"Then keep away!" I said.

They pushed again, and I struck out with my right and caught him in the mouth. The crowd shouted and pushed us. I fought like a dog. I knew that if I did not

---

noon, 12 o'clock in the day

win, I would have to fight a new boy every day. The bell rang. Neither of us had won the fight.

In the classroom, the boys asked me questions about myself. I was someone worth knowing. When the bell rang at the end of the school day, I was ready to fight again; but the boy was not to be seen.

No sooner had I won my right to the schoolyard than a new fear arose. One evening before bedtime, I was sitting in the front room, reading. Uncle Clark was at his table, drawing, and Aunt Jody was making a shirt. The doorbell rang, and Aunt Jody answered it. The visitor was one of the neighbors, Mr Burden. I rose and shook his hand.

"Well, son," Mr Burden told me, "it's certainly nice to see another boy in this house."

"Is there another boy here?" I asked.

"My son was here," said Mr Burden. "We used to live in this house. But he's gone now."

"How old is he?"

"He was about your age," Mr Burden said.

"Where did he go?" I asked.

"He's dead," Mr Burden said.

"Oh," I said.

I had not understood him. Nobody said anything for a long time.

"Do you sleep in there?" asked Mr Burden, pointing to my room.

"Yes, sir."

"That's where my boy slept," he said.

"In **there?**" I asked.

"Yes, right in there."

"On **that** bed?" I asked.

"Yes, that was his bed. When I heard you were

coming, I gave your uncle that bed for you," he explained.

After Mr Burden had gone, I went to Uncle Clark.

"I'm afraid to sleep in there," I told him.

"Why? Because a boy died in there?"

"Yes, sir."

"But, son, that's nothing to be afraid of."

"I know, but I am afraid."

"It'll pass. You'll get over it."

"But can't I sleep somewhere else?"

"There's nowhere else for you to sleep."

"May I sleep here, on the sofa?"

"No," Aunt Jody said.

I went into the dark room and put out my hand to find the bed. I felt that if I touched the bed I would find the dead boy in it. Finally I jumped into the bed and pulled the covers over my face. I did not sleep that night, and my eyes were red the next morning.

"Didn't you sleep well?" Uncle Clark asked me.

"I can't sleep in that room," I said.

"You slept in it before you heard of that boy who died in there, didn't you?" Aunt Jody asked me.

"Yes, *ma'am*."

"Then why can't you sleep in it now?"

"I'm afraid."

"You stop being a baby," she told me.

The next night was the same; fear kept me from sleeping. After Uncle Clark and Aunt Jody had gone to bed, I rose and crept into the front room and slept on the sofa. I woke in the morning to find Uncle Clark shaking me.

---

ma'am (madam), Mrs, lady

"Why are you doing this?" he asked.

"I'm afraid to sleep in there," I said.

"You go back into that room and sleep tonight," he told me. "You must get over this thing."

"Uncle Clark, send me back to Jackson," I said.

"You're not happy here?"

"No, sir," I answered.

"And you really want to go back?"

"Yes, sir."

"Things will not be easy for you at home. There's not too much money for food," he said.

"I want to be where my mother is," I said.

"But what about school?"

"I don't care."

"All right," he said. "I'll send you home on Saturday."

* * *

I was glad to see my mother. She was much better, though still in bed. The doctor had said she must have an operation. Uncle Edward came from Carters to take my mother to Clarksdale for the operation. At the last moment, I said I wanted to go with them. We said very little during the trip. When we came to the doctor's room, I was sure that my mother would never be well again. The doctor took her inside. Uncle Edward and I waited. Hours later, the doctor came out of the door.

"How's my mother?"

"Fine!" he said.

"Can I see her now?"

"No, not now."

Uncle Edward had gone out to get a room and a

nurse for my mother. He returned with an ambulance and two men. They entered the doctor's room and brought out my mother.

"Why are they taking Mama that way?"

"The hospitals are not for colored people, and this is the way we have to do it."

They lifted my mother into the ambulance and drove away. I knew she had gone out of my life. I could feel it.

She remained in bed ten years, growing better little by little, but never really well. The family had got together all the money they could get, and there was no more to do anything with.

---

nurse, woman who looks after sick people

4

Aunt Addie, Granny's youngest child, was the only teacher at the religious school, and that was where I was sent. From the first day, Aunt Addie and I were enemies. She had not taught before, and she did not like having a member of her family in her classroom. At the end of the first week, open war broke out between us.

One afternoon she rose from her desk and walked down the classroom and stopped beside me.

"Look at that floor!" she said.

I looked and saw little bits of *walnut* on the clean floor.

"I don't know anything about that," I said.

"You know better than to eat in the classroom."

"I haven't been eating," I said.

"Don't lie!"

"Aunt Addie, my walnuts are here in my pocket."

"I'm Miss Wilson!"

I looked at her. She had told me to call her Miss Wilson in the classroom, and usually I did.

"I'm sorry," I said.

"Richard, get up!"

I did not move. I had not eaten the walnuts, and I did not want to be beaten for it. I hoped that the boy in front of me would save me. He was the one who had done it.

"I asked you to get up!" Aunt Addie shouted.

"I haven't done anything!" I said.

"Go to the front of the room," she said.

I walked slowly to her desk.

She struck me. I moved away.

"Stand still, boy!"

I stood still.

"Hold out your hand!"

I held out my hand, and she struck me until the hand was red.

"Put down your hand and go to your seat," she said.

I sat down. I was sure of one thing: I would not be beaten by her again. I knew I had been beaten for a reason that was not right. All afternoon I was wondering how I could leave the school.

The moment Aunt Addie came into the house, she called me into the kitchen. When I entered, I saw that she was holding a stick.

"You're not going to beat me again!" I told her. "You beat me for throwing walnuts on the floor! But I didn't do it!"

"Then who did?"

I told her the name of the boy.

"Why didn't you tell me before?" she asked.

"I don't want to tell tales on other people."

"So you lied?"

I could not talk.

"Hold out your hand."

"You're not going to beat me."

"I'm going to beat you for lying."

For a moment she waited, then she struck at me with the stick and I fell into a corner. She was upon me. I jumped up, and opened a *drawer*; it fell to the

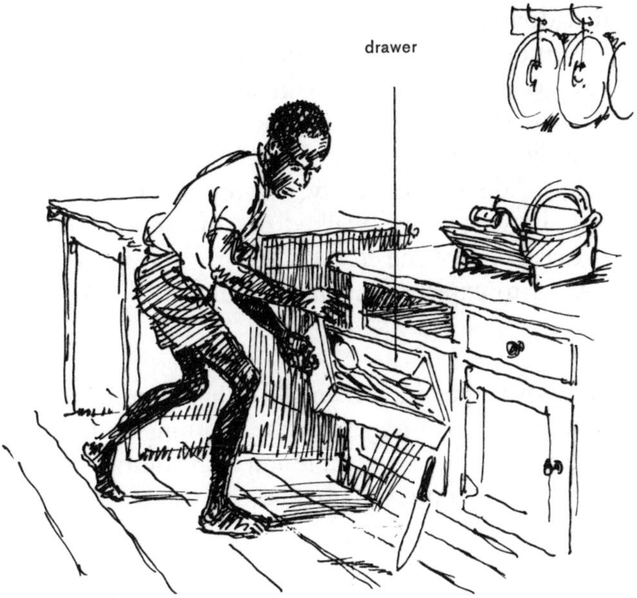

floor with a loud noise. I took a knife and held it up.

"Now, I told you to stop!" I shouted.

"You put down that knife!"

"Leave me alone, or I'll cut you!"

She stood still, then she made up her mind and came at me. I hit out with the knife and she took my hand and tried to take the knife. I threw my right leg behind her, and we fell to the floor. She was stronger than I, and she was still trying to get the knife.

"Leave me alone!" I shouted.

"Give me that knife, boy!"

"I'll kill you! I'll kill you if you don't leave me alone!"

Granny came running.

"Addie! What are you doing?"

"He's got a knife!" said Aunt Addie. "Make him put it down!"

My mother came to the door.

"Richard, put down that knife!" she shouted.

"I won't! I'm not going to let her beat me."

"Addie! Leave the boy alone," my mother said.

Aunt Addie rose slowly, her eyes on the knife. Then she turned and walked out of the kitchen.

"Richard, give me that knife," my mother said.

I tried to explain, but they would not listen.

* * *

Granny was the oldest member of her church, and in the house we had *prayers* in the morning and in the evening, at the breakfast table and at the dinner table. I did not go to church as often as she wanted me to; I

---

prayers, talks with God

said I had no time and had to study for school. Every day I went to my room, and tried to pray, but it was no use. I could not pray. So, to pass the time in my room, I took the Bible, *pencil* and paper, and tried to write *hymns.* But that was no good either.

One day, during my hour of prayer, I remembered some Indian history books that I had read the year before. Yes, I knew what I would do; I would write a story about the Indians ... But what about them? Well, an Indian girl ... I wrote of a young Indian girl, beautiful and good, who sat alone by the side of a river, waiting ... Not knowing how to go on, I decided that the girl had to die. She rose slowly and walked into the dark water, and walked on until the water reached her neck; then it covered her. Not a sound came from her, even in dying.

I read the story over and saw that it was no good. But I had never in my life done anything like it; I had made something, no matter how bad it was; and it was mine ... Now, to whom could I show it? I decided to read the story to a young woman who lived next door. When I had finished, she smiled at me in a strange way.

"What's that for?" she asked.

"Nothing," I said.

"But why did you write it?"

"I just wanted to."

"Where did you get the idea?"

pencil

---

hymn, song used in church

"Oh, I don't know. I just thought it up."

"What are you going to do with it?"

"Nothing."

I never forgot the look of surprise on the young woman's face. But for some reason I felt pleased whenever I thought of it.

5

I went to school, wanting to learn but also to get into another world of people. The first day at the Jim Hill school, I walked into the schoolyard wearing a new *straw hat.* I hoped nobody would notice me. But I knew that sooner or later somebody would find out that I was a new boy. A black boy ran past me, threw the straw hat to the ground, and shouted:

"Straw hat!"

I picked up the hat and another boy ran past, pushed my hat off my head, and shouted:

"Straw hat!"

Again I picked up my hat and waited. The cry spread. Boys gathered around me, pointing, calling:

"Straw hat! Straw hat!"

"Where are you from?" a boy asked me.

"None of your business," I said.

"Now, you be careful, or I'll cut you down," he said.

"I'll say what I please."

The boy picked up a small stone, put it on his shoulder and walked up close to me.

I waited a moment; then I pushed the stone from his shoulder, bent down, put my arms round his legs and brought him down. I jumped upon him and started hitting him. Then I was pulled up, and another boy began to fight me.

"Don't hit my brother!" he shouted.

Both of them closed in on me. A blow landed on the back of my head. I turned round and saw a stone rolling away, and I felt blood running down my back. The two boys stepped back. One of them turned and ran. I threw a stone and hit him in the middle of his back. I ran after the other, while the boys crowded round me. Suddenly they all moved away. I saw a woman teacher coming fast towards me.

"Was it you who threw that stone?" she asked.

"Two boys were fighting me," I told her.

"Come," she said, taking my hand.

I was taken to a room with the two brothers.

"Are these the boys?"

"Both of them fought me, and they tore up my new hat."

"He hit me first!" one of them shouted.

"You're lying!" I cried back

The teacher ordered me to sit down; I did, but kept my eyes on the two brothers. The teacher took them out of the room, and I sat still until she came back.

She asked me my name and sent me to a room. For a reason I could not understand, they put me in the fifth *grade*. Would they find out that I did not belong there? I sat and waited. When I was asked my age I called it out. Then they said I could stay.

I studied day and night, and in two weeks I was put in the sixth grade. The family had not thought it possible. How could a bad, bad boy do that?

I was now with boys and girls who were studying, fighting, talking. I knew I was in the middle of a new world. This was a world that I had to fight and meet when I grew up. Suddenly I could see the future before me, as much of a future as there is for a black boy in Mississippi.

I did not tell the boys and girls at school much about my home. Because my home was so poor, I was kept out of the world in which the other boys and girls lived. I did not want them to know this. Every day at noon I would follow the boys into the store at the corner of the street and stand against the wall and watch them eat *sandwiches*. When they would ask me: "Why don't you eat a lunch?" I would answer: "Oh, I'm not hungry at noon, ever."

I now saw a world come to life before my eyes. I

sandwich

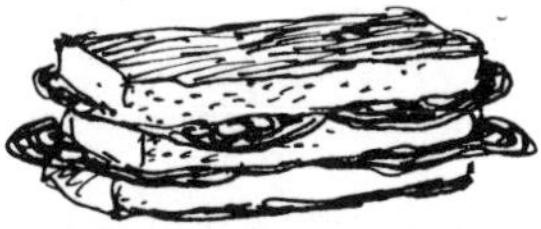

---

grade, class or year

could go out and watch it, because I did not go home when school was over. If I went home to eat, Granny would not allow me out again. With my books over my shoulder, I went out with my friends into the woods, to the river, to business streets, to the *movies* when we could get in without paying. I was happy to be free. I didn't care if I had to go without food for twelve hours.

* * *

In my class was a tall, black boy who was very bright in his studies. It was he who found out that I was always hungry. He told me a way to make money.

"You can't sit in school all day and not eat," he said.

"What am I going to eat?" I asked.

"Why don't you do like me?"

"What do you do?"

"I sell papers."

"I'd like to sell papers, because I could read them. I can't find things to read."

"You too?" he asked, laughing.

"What do you mean?" I asked.

"That's why I sell papers. I like to read them, and that's the only way I can get hold of them," he explained.

"What kind of a paper are you selling?"

"It comes from Chicago. I only read the stories in the magazine part of the paper. I'm reading the *serial* of *Zane Grey*'s Riders of the Purple Sage."

---

movie, film
serial, story in short parts, often once a week
Zane Grey (1872-1939), American writer, known for his books about cowboys in the U.S. West

I could not believe him. I just stared at him.
"Riders of the Purple Sage!" I cried.
"Yes."
"Do you think I can sell those papers?"
"Sure. I make over fifty cents a week and have stories to read," he explained.
I followed him home and he showed me one of the newspapers.
"Hurry up and start selling them. I'd like to talk to you about the stories."
I promised that I would order some papers the same night. I walked home reading, lifting my eyes now and then in order not to run into anybody.
The papers arrived, and I soon sold a number of them. People bought them more because they knew me than because they wanted to read. When I returned home in the evening I would go to my room and read. The stories were not very good, but I wanted to believe them. They were my doorway to another world.
One day I came to the house of a friend of the family.
"You know, son," he said, "I do like to see you make a little money every week."
"Thank you, sir," I said.
"But tell me, who told you to sell these papers?"
"Nobody."
"Where do you get them from?"
"Chicago."
"Do you ever read them?"
"Sure. I read the stories in the magazine part. But I never read the rest of the newspaper."
"Did a white man ask you to sell these papers?"

"No, sir. Why do you ask?"

He did not answer. He was sitting outside the house. He got up slowly.

"Wait here a minute. I want to show you something."

He entered the house, and came back with one of the newspapers. He handed it to me.

"Well, just take a look at this. Take your time and tell me what you think."

I took the paper from him, sat down and read, turning the pages. I read things so anti-Negro that they felt like cold water being poured down my back.

"Did you ever hear of the Ku Klux Klan?" the man asked me softly.

"Sure. Why?"

"Do you know what the Ku Kluxers do to colored people?"

"They kill us. They keep us from voting and getting good jobs," I said.

"Well, the paper you're selling is full of Ku Klux Klan writings," he said.

"Oh, no!" I exclaimed.

"Son, you're holding it in your hands," he said.

"I read the magazine, but I never read the paper," I said uncertainly.

"Listen, son," he said. "You're a black boy and you're trying to make a few pennies. All right. But I've read these papers now for two months and I know what they are trying to do. If you sell them, you're just helping white people to kill you. Do you like that?"

"No, sir," I breathed.

"Are you going to sell those papers now?"

"No, sir. Never again."

I walked home with the papers under my arm, feeling that some Negro would jump upon me from behind the corner of a house.

The father of the boy who told me to sell the newspapers also found out about them. He told his son not to sell them. One day the boy asked me:

"Are you still selling those papers?"

"Oh, no, I don't have time," I said, but I didn't look at him.

"Nor do I," he said. "I'm too busy."

* * *

I studied very hard. When school began, I read my books through. Then I only looked in them again when in class. I did all my mathematics a long time before I was asked to. Then during school hours, when I was not asked to speak, I read stories. Sometimes I dreamed about cities I had never seen and about people I had never met.

I came in from school one afternoon and Aunt Addie met me in the hall.

"Go up and say goodbye to Grandpa," she said.

"What's happened?"

She did not answer. I ran up the stairs and met Uncle Clark, who had come from Greenwood. Granny caught my hand.

"Come and say goodbye to Grandpa."

She led me to Grandpa's room. He was lying on the bed, looking as well as he ever looked. His eyes were open, but he was very still. He was so still that I did not know if he was dead or alive.

"Papa, here's Richard," Granny whispered.

Grandpa looked at me.

"Goodbye, Grandpa," I whispered.

"Goodbye, son," he said. "Be happy, for God has chosen my s-s-ea ... in h-heaven ..."

His voice died. I had not understood what he had said. I wondered if I should ask him to say it again. But Granny took my hand and led me from the room.

"Granny, what did Grandpa say? I didn't quite hear him."

"Shut up. Death is in the house."

"I just wanted to know," I said.

She looked at me.

"He said that God had chosen his seat in heaven,"

she said.

When I woke up the next morning, my mother told me that Grandpa had "gone home".

* * *

My clothes were becoming so old that I did not want to go to school in them. Many of the boys in the class were wearing their first *long-pants suits.* I decided to tell Granny what I wanted to do. I wanted to work on Saturdays. If she did not let me work on Saturdays, then I would leave home. But when I tried to speak to her, she would not listen. I followed her about the house. Her answer was no and no and no.

"Then I'll leave school," I said.

"Do as you like. I don't care."

"I'll go away from here and you'll never hear from me!"

"No, you won't."

"How can I ever learn enough to get a job?" I asked her. I showed her my clothes. "Look, I won't go to school like this. I'm not asking you for money or to do anything. I only want to work!"

"I have nothing to do with whether you go to school or not," she said. "If you will not ask God for

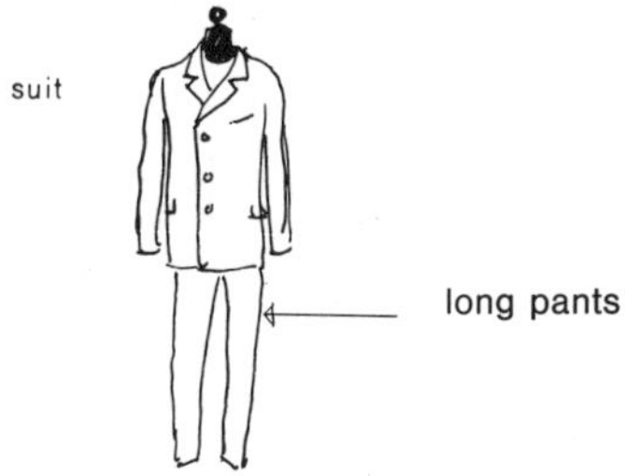

help, I can't help you. You're dead to me, dead to Christ."

"I'm going to get a job anyway."

"Then you can't live here."

"Then I'll leave," I said, my whole body shaking.

"You won't leave," she repeated.

"I'll leave this minute!"

I ran to my room, and began packing my things. I did not have a penny, but I was going to leave. Granny came to the door.

"You little fool! Put down that bag!"

"I'm going where I can work!"

She took the bag out of my hands. "All right," she said. "If you want to go to *hell*, then go. God will forgive me, but he won't forgive you."

Her face wet with tears, she ran away from the door. Now I was truly dead to Granny and Aunt Addie. But my mother smiled when I told her that I had stood up against them. She rose and walked slowly over to me and kissed me.

---

hell, a hot place where bad people are said to go when they die

6

Summer. Bright hot days. Hunger. Will I be able to enter school in September? Reading. Looking for jobs. Hope of going North. But what would become of my mother if I left her? Doubt. Fear.

Word came that a *brickyard* wanted men, and I went to find out. I walked into the yard and came to a *barrow* full of new bricks. I could not even lift it.

Later I found that they wanted a water boy. I ran to the office and got the job. In the hot sun I carried a big pail from one gang of black men to another, giving them water to drink, earning a dollar a day. I would call out:

"Water!"

And somebody would shout:

"Here, boy!"

Almost falling down with hunger, I would carry the

brickyard, factory where bricks are made for building houses

pail around. Then, at the end of the week, the money would go on all the things we had to buy at home.

Later I got a job in the yard that paid a dollar and a half a day. I went between the walls of new bricks and picked up those which had turned out bad, and took them away in a barrow. Then the brickyard closed.

School opened again. I went to classes without books for a month. Then I got a job working mornings and evenings for three dollars a week.

One long afternoon I took some paper and told myself I would write a story. Only, what would the story be about? Finally, I wrote as I felt. The story was about a bad man who wanted to steal an old woman's house. I finished the story in three days and then wondered what to do with it.

The Negro newspaper of the town! That's it ... I sailed into the office and put the story under the nose of the man who called himself the *editor*.

"What is that?" he asked.

"A story," I said.

"All right. I'll read it."

He pushed my pages back on his desk and looked at me.

"But I want you to read it now," I said.

"I'll read this and let you know about it tomorrow," he said.

"Give me the story," I said, putting out my hand.

He turned from me, took up the book, and read ten pages or more.

"Won't you come in tomorrow?" he asked. "I'll

---

editor, person working for the newspaper who decides what is to be printed

have it finished then."

"All right," I said. "I'll come back tomorrow."

The next afternoon, on my way to work, I stepped into the newspaper office.

"Where is my story?" I asked.

"It is being printed," he said.

"How much money will I get?" I asked, nearly jumping up and down.

"We can't pay you for it."

"But you sell your papers for money," I said.

"Look, you're just starting. This story will put your name before our readers. Now, that's something," he said.

"But if the story is good enough to sell to your readers, then you ought to give me some of the money you get from it."

He laughed.

"I'm going to give you something that's better than money. I'll give you a chance to learn to write."

I was pleased, but still I didn't like it.

"What are you doing this summer?"

"Nothing."

"Then come to see me before you take another job," he said. "And write some more stories."

A few days later, my friends in the class came to me and showed me the newspaper.

"Did you really write that story?" they asked me.

"Yes."

"Why?"

"Because I wanted to," I said.

"Where did you get it from?" they asked.

"I made it up."

"But what have they printed it for?"

"So people can read it."

"Who told you to do that?"

"Nobody."

"Then why did you do it?"

"Because I wanted to," I said again.

They were sure I was not telling them the truth. We had never learned to write stories at school.

At home it was the same thing. Granny came into my room early one morning and sat down on my bed.

"Richard, what is this you're putting in the papers?" she asked.

"A story."

"About what?"

"It's just a story, Granny."

"But they tell me it has been in three times."

"It's the same story. It's in three parts."

"But what is it about?" she wanted to know again.

"It's just a story I made up," I said.

"Then it's a lie," she said.

"Oh, Christ," I said.

"You must get out of this house if you say such things," she said.

"Granny, please ... I'm sorry. But it's hard to tell you about the story. You see, Granny, everybody knows that the story isn't true, but ..."

"Then why write it?"

"Because people might want to read it."

My mother was also troubled.

"Son, you should not do such silly things. Suppose they wanted you to teach here in Jackson? Then, suppose they found out that you had been writing stories?"

I could not answer her.

"I'll be all right, Mama," I said.

Uncle Tom didn't like the story. Aunt Addie said it was wrong to use the words I had put in it.

In the end I was so angry that I refused to talk about the story. I was angry that the people around me did not like the story and did not want me to write more. I did not understand, then, that by trying to write I was pushing against the whole way of life of the South.

I dreamed of going North and writing books, *novels.* To me the North was all that I had not felt or seen. I was wise enough not to hope to become rich. I knew that I lived in a country where a black man could not do all he wanted. Yet I felt I had to go somewhere and do something to pay up for being

---

novel, book with only one long story in it

alive. I was beginning to dream dreams that the state had said were wrong, that the schools had said were wrong. My friends at school felt I was doing something that was wrong; but they were not able to express it.

7

Summer again. The old problem of looking for a job. I was working part of the time in the house of a white woman called Mrs Bibbs. I told her that I wanted a job. I needed enough money to buy clothes and books for the next school year. She took the matter up with her husband, who worked in a *sawmill*.

"So you want to work in the mill?"

"Yes, sir."

He came to me and put his hands under my arms and lifted me from the floor.

"You're too light for our work," he said.

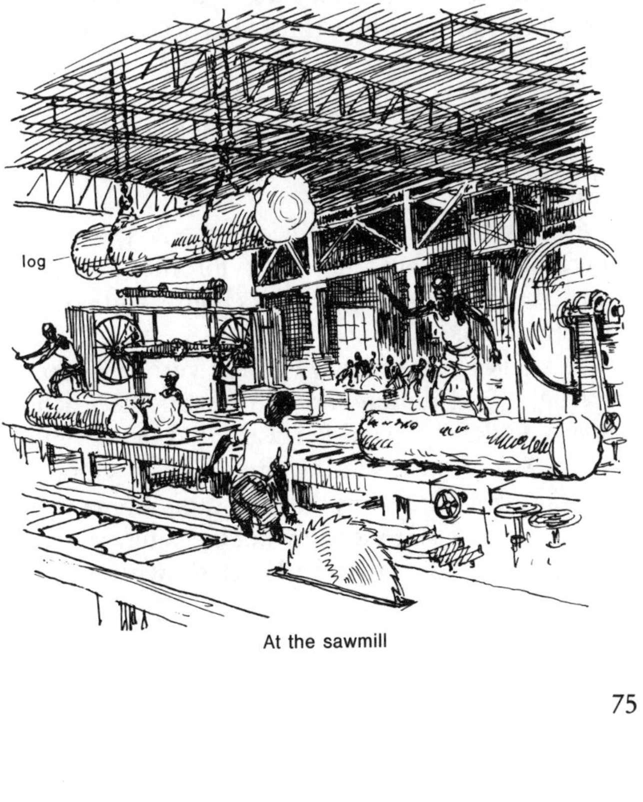

At the sawmill

But I did not leave the room. My standing still there was a way of asking him to think it over again. I was telling him that I wanted a job in his mill. "All right," he said finally. "Come to the mill in the morning. I'll see what I can do."

I was at the mill in the morning, and saw the men lifting heavy *logs*.

"Watch out!" somebody shouted.

I looked around and saw a black man pointing above my head. A log was swinging towards me. I ran clear. The black man came to my side.

"What do you want here, boy?"

"I'm looking for a job."

"I wouldn't try for this if I were you." He held up his right hand from which three fingers were missing. "See?"

I left.

Empty days. Long days. Bright hot days. I spent the mornings looking for jobs, and I read in the afternoons.

One day I went to the office of the Negro newspaper, but there was no work for me. Finally I returned to my job at Mrs Bibbs's house, and bought my schoolbooks.

The studies in the ninth – my last year at school – were light; and during part of the year the teacher made me take the class. If I was good, it was said, perhaps I could teach in the city school system.

During that winter my brother came home from Chicago. I was glad to see him, but the family showed him more love than they had ever shown me.

---

log: see picture, page 75

The school year ended. I was chosen to speak for my class. I was told to write my *speech*. One morning, the *principal* called me to his office.

"Well, Richard Wright, here's your speech," he said and pushed some papers across his table.

"What speech?" I asked as I picked up the papers.

"The speech you're going to say on the night of *graduation*," he said.

"But, professor, I've written my speech already," I said.

He laughed at me in a friendly way.

"Listen, boy. You're going to speak to both white and colored people that night. What can you alone think of saying to them?"

"I know that I'm only a boy, professor. But the people come to hear the students, and I won't make a speech that you've written."

He leaned back in his chair and looked at me in surprise.

"You know, we've never had a boy in this school like you before," he said. "You've done things the way you want to around here, I don't know how. But, listen, you take this speech and say it. I know what's best for you. I have seen many a boy and girl graduate from this school, and none of them was too proud to say a speech I wrote for them."

"Professor, I'm going to say my own speech that night," I said.

He grew angry. "Suppose you don't graduate?"

---

speech, words spoken (or written down to be spoken)
principal, head of the school
graduation, leaving school after passing an exam (verb: *graduate*)

“I have passed my examinations,” I said.

“Look, mister,” he shot at me, “I’m the one who says who passes at this school.”

“Then I don’t graduate,” I said flatly.

I turned to leave.

“Say, you. Come here,” he called.

I turned and looked at him; he was smiling at me, in a distant sort of way.

“You know, I’m glad I talked to you,” he said. “I was going to place you in the school system, teaching. But now, I don’t think that you will fit.”

“Look, professor, I may never get a chance to go to school again,” I said. “But I like to do things right.”

“What do you mean?”

"I've no money. I'm going to work, and this *diploma* isn't going to help me much in life. I'm not bitter about it. But I'm just not going to do things this way."

"Have you talked to anybody about this?"

"No, why?"

"Are you sure?"

"This is the first I've heard of it, professor."

"You haven't talked to any white people about this?"

"No, sir!"

Now I began to understand; the man was afraid now for his job.

"Now, if you do as I say, I'll help you to go to *college*."

"I want to learn, professor," I told him. "But there are some things I don't want to know."

"Goodbye," he said.

I went home. I had been talking to a "bought" man, and he had tried to "buy" me. That night Griggs, a boy who had gone through many classes with me, came to the house.

"Look, Dick, you're throwing away your future

---

college, school for young people 17 to 22 years of age

here in Jackson," he said. "Go to the principal, talk to him, take his speech, and say it. I'm saying the speech he wrote. So why can't you? What can you lose?"

"No," I said.

"Why?"

"I know very little, but my speech is going to show that," I said.

"Then they won't take you on as a teacher."

"Who said I was going to teach?" I asked.

He left. Two days later Uncle Tom came to me. I knew that the principal had called him in.

"I hear that the principal wants you to say a speech. And you have refused to say it," he said.

"Yes, sir. That's right," I said.

"May I read the speech you've written?"

"Certainly," I said.

"And may I see the one the principal wrote?"

I gave him the principal's speech too. He went to his room to read them both. I sat quiet, waiting. He returned.

"The principal's speech is the better speech," he said.

"I don't doubt it," I replied. "But why did they ask me to write a speech if I can't say it?"

"Would you let me work on your speech?" he said.

"No, sir."

"Now look, Richard, this is your future ..."

"Uncle Tom, I don't want to talk about this with you."

He left. The principal's speech was clearer than mine, but it said nothing. Mine was not so clear, but it said what I wanted to say. What could I do?

Griggs had accepted a speech written by the

principal. He came to my house every day, and we went off into the woods to say the speeches over. Day in and day out we spoke to the trees. Finally I could have said my speech in my sleep.

My friends in the class had heard what had happened and said:

"Richard, you are a fool. They didn't know you were such a fool when they asked you to write a speech."

My friends were trying to "save" me. I asked them to shut up. In the end the principal had to order them to leave me alone. He was afraid that I would just walk out.

On the night of graduation I was nervous. I got up and my speech rolled out. When my voice stopped, some people clapped their hands. I did not care if they liked it or not. A few of my friends shook hands with me before I left the hall. Somebody asked me to a party, but I did not go. I did not want to see any of them again. I walked home.

8

It was important for me now to find work, and I accepted the first offer. This was a job in a store that sold clothes to Negroes *on credit.* The shop was always full of black men and women who paid any price the white man asked.

One morning, while I was cleaning windows, the *boss* and his son drove up in their car. A black woman sat between them. They got out and half kicked and half pulled the woman into the store. White people passed and looked on without saying a word. A white policeman watched from the corner, but he made no move. After a moment or two I heard screams coming from a room in the store. Later the woman walked out crying, her clothes torn. When she was in the street, the policeman went up to her, took hold of her, said she was drunk, called a police car and had her taken away.

When I went into the store, the boss and his son were washing their hands. They looked at me and laughed. There was blood and hair on the floor.

"Boy, that's what we do to niggers when they don't pay," the boss said.

His son looked at me.

"Here, have a cigarette," he said.

Not knowing what to do, I took the cigarette. He lit it for me. This was a way of telling me how things lay between us: even if they had beaten the black woman, they would not beat me if I kept my mouth shut.

---

on credit, so that they could pay later
boss, person in charge

"Yes, sir," I said.

After they had gone, I sat on a box and looked at the floor until the cigarette went out.

The store owned a bicycle which I used in taking goods to the customers. One day I had a *puncture* on my way back from outside town. I walked along the hot road, leading the bicycle beside me.

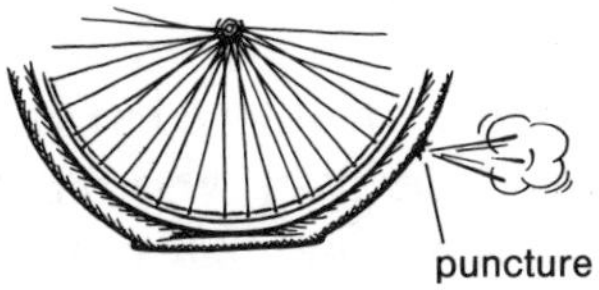

A car came up to me.

"What's the matter there, boy?" a white man called.

I told him that my bicycle was broken and that I was walking back to town.

"That's too bad," he said. "Hop on the *running board.*"

He stopped the car. I held the bicycle with one hand and held on to the car with the other.

"All right?"

"Yes, sir."

The car started. It was full of young white men. They were drinking.

"Want a drink, boy?" one asked.

"Oh, no!" I said.

I had hardly said the words when I felt something hard hit me between the eyes. It was an empty whisky bottle. I saw stars, and fell off the car on top of the bicycle. The car stopped, and the white men came out and stood over me.

"Nigger, haven't you learned to say 'sir' to a white man yet?" asked the man who hit me.

I got on my feet. The man came towards me.

"Oh, leave him alone, he's got enough," said one.

"You want to come back to town, nigger?"

"I want to walk," I said.

Before they got back into the car they said:

"Nigger, you ought to be glad it was us you talked to that way. If you said that to some other white man, you might be a dead nigger now."

I hated the way they treated Negroes in the clothes store, and they saw it, and sent me away.

* * *

I had a number of small jobs, each for a short time. Then one day a friend told me that the only Negro movie house wanted a boy to take tickets at the door. The Jewish owner accepted me at once, and the next day I began taking tickets. The boss said:

"Now, look, I'll be *honest* with you if you'll be honest with me. I don't know who is honest here and who isn't. But if **you** are honest, then the rest must be

---

honest, not lying or stealing

honest too. All tickets will pass through your hands. Nobody can steal if you don't steal."

During the first afternoon, the Negro girl in the ticket office watched me. I knew she was trying to see if I was honest or if she could use me.

When I had taken a ticket from a customer I dropped it into a box. Sometimes the boss would go to the ticket window and look at the numbers and then look at the number of the ticket I had just dropped in the box. After a few days the boss began to watch me from across the street, and finally he stayed away for hours at a time.

While I was eating in a nearby café one night, a Negro man walked in and sat beside me.

"Hello, Richard," he said.

"Hello," I said. "I don't think I know you."

"But I know you," he said.

"How do you know me?" I asked.

"I'm Tel's friend," he said, naming the girl who sold the tickets at the movie.

I looked at him. Was he telling me the truth?

"We start tonight," he said.

"What?" I asked.

"Don't be afraid. The boss knows you are honest. He has gone to see some friends. Somebody is watching him. If he starts back to the movie, they'll phone us," he said.

I was so afraid I could not eat my food.

"It'll work this way," he explained. "A man will come to you and ask for a cigarette. You give him five tickets that you take out of the box, see? We'll give you the signal when to start. The man'll give the tickets to Tel; she'll sell them again at once. You understand?"

I did not answer. I knew one thing: if I were caught, the police would take me away, for years of hard labor. But was not my life already a kind of hard labor? What, really, did I have to lose?

"Are you with us?" he asked.

I still did not answer. He rose and put his hand on

my shoulder and left. Anything might happen, but I was used to that. I went back to the theater.

I took the tickets. I waited.

The man I had met in the café came through the door and put a ticket in my hand.

"There's a crowd at the ticket office," he said. "Take ten, not five. Start with this one."

Well, here goes, I thought. He gave me the ticket and sat looking at the movie. After a moment another black man came up to me.

"Got a cigarette?"

I gave him the tickets. He went out to the ticket office and I saw him give the tickets to the girl. She smiled at me and I went back inside. A few moments later the same tickets were handed to me by other customers.

We worked it for a week. After the money was divided into four parts, I had fifty dollars. I tried to say to Tel's friend that maybe I would leave, but that made him very angry.

I went through another week. Late one night, I decided to make that week the last. I broke into the neighbor's house and stole his gun. I found two boys to help me, and we broke into a store and stole *cans* of fruit. Then we sold the cans to restaurants. I bought clothes, shoes, and a bag, and hid the things at home.

cans

Saturday night came, and I sent word to the boss that I was ill. Uncle Tom was in his room. Granny and Aunt Addie were at church. My brother was sleeping. I packed my bag, and went to my mother.

"Mama, I'm going away," I whispered.

"Oh, no," she said.

"I've got to, Mama. I can't live this way."

"You're not running away from something you've done?"

"I'll send for you, Mama. I'll be all right."

"Take care of yourself. And send for me quickly. I'm not happy here," she said.

"I'm sorry for all these long years, Mama. But I could not have helped it."

I kissed her and she cried.

"Be quiet, Mama. I'm all right."

I went out the back way and walked ten minutes to the station. I bought my ticket, then went back to the corner near the movie house. Yes, the boss was there, taking the tickets himself. I returned to the station and waited for my train, my eyes watching the crowd.

An hour later I was on my way towards the North. This was the first part of my journey to a land where I could live with a little less fear.

Well, it's my life, I told myself. I'll see what I can make of it ...

9

I arrived in Memphis on a cold November Sunday morning. After walking through several streets I saw a big house with a sign in the window: Rooms. I walked up the steps. I was about to ring the bell when I saw a big Negro woman looking at me through the window.

"Come here, boy," she called.

I looked at her a moment, then stepped into a warm hall.

She said, "I'm Mrs Moss."

I told her my name.

"We take in people to live here. We are just simple people. You can call this home if you want to. The room is three dollars."

I accepted and she showed me the room.

"You ran off, didn't you?"

I looked at her in surprise.

"How did you know?"

"Boy, your heart's like an open book," she said. "I know things. You drink?"

"Oh, no, ma'am."

"Just wanted to know. You can drink here if you like. You can bring your girl here too. Only be a good boy."

I sat on the bed and looked at her. Here, in this bad street, I had met the warmest, most friendly person I had ever known.

One summer morning I was washing a pair of *eyeglasses* in the factory where I worked. The

---

eyeglasses: see picture, page 90

machines were working around me. It was near noon and I was thinking of lunch. Mr Olin, the white foreman under whom I worked, came up to me.

"Boy, how's it going?" he asked.

"Oh, fine, sir!" I answered.

"Say, Richard, do you believe that I'm your friend?"

I knew that all white men in the South thought themselves the friends of niggers. While thinking of an answer that would say nothing, I smiled.

"I mean," he went on, "do you think I'm your friend?"

"Well," I answered. "I hope you are."

"I am," he said.

I went on with my work.

"I want to tell you something," he said.

"Yes, sir," I said.

"We like you round here; you act like a good boy. We don't want you to get hurt."

"Yes, sir," I said. "What's wrong?"

He lit a cigarette. "Do you know Harrison?"

He was speaking of a boy of about my own age who worked across the street for another factory.

"Yes, sir," I said. "I know him."

"Well, be careful. He's after you."

"After me? For what?"

"I don't know. What have you done to him?"

I forgot what I was doing. My eyes were upon Mr Olin's face, trying to see what he meant. I did not trust

eyeglasses

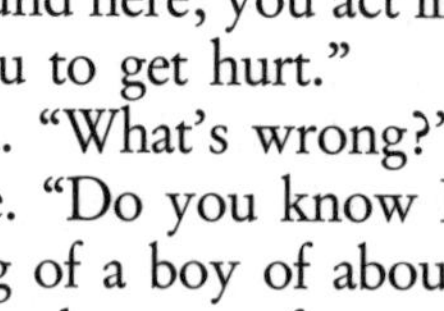

the white man, nor did I trust Harrison. Who was my friend: the white man or the black boy?

"Well, you had better look out. A little while ago, I went down to get a Coca-Cola; and Harrison was waiting for you at the door with a knife in his hand. Said he was going to get you."

"I've got to see that boy and talk to him," I said.

"You had better not," Mr Olin said. "You had better let some of us white boys talk to him. I'll take care of it."

At noon I went across the street and found Harrison sitting on a box inside the door. He was having lunch. As I came up to him, he put his hand in his pocket and looked at me.

"Say, Harrison, what's all this about?" I asked, standing four feet from him.

He looked at me a long time and didn't answer.

"I haven't done anything to you," I said.

"And I haven't got anything against you," he answered.

"But Mr Olin said that you came over this morning, looking for me with a knife."

"Oh, no," he said. "I haven't been in your factory all day."

"Then what did Mr Olin mean?" I asked.

"I thought you were looking for me," Harrison explained. "Mr Olin came over here this morning and said you were going to kill me. He said you were angry because I had said something about you. But I have said nothing about you." He got up.

"Look here, don't believe what Mr Olin says."

"I see now," Harrison said. "He was trying to make us kill each other. But why should he do that?"

"I suppose it's fun for white men to see niggers fight," I said.

At one o'clock I went back to the factory. Mr Olin was waiting for me.

"Did you see that Harrison nigger?" he asked.

"No, sir," I lied.

"Well, he still has that knife for you. Did you buy a knife?"

"No, sir," I answered.

"Do you want to use mine?" he asked.

He laid an open knife beside my hand. I put the knife in my pocket.

I was afraid to look at him. I knew what he was trying to do. And if I looked at him, I would have to tell him that I knew. I said nothing. He was my boss.

In the afternoon, I stole a few minutes to run across the street to talk to Harrison. He told me that Mr Olin had telephoned his boss. The boss had told Harrison that I planned to wait for him at 6 o'clock and kill him. We told ourselves again and again that we did not believe the white men. Yet deep down in us there was a fear that it might be true.

"I wish they would leave us alone," I said.

"Me too," Harrison said.

"There are a million black boys who could do our jobs," I said. "They wouldn't care if we killed each other."

"I know it," Harrison said.

* * *

One morning a few days later, Mr Olin and a group of white men came to me. They asked me if I was willing to fight Harrison with *gloves.* I told them I was

not afraid of Harrison, but I did not want to fight him. I added that I did not know how to box. I could feel that they knew that I no longer believed them.

When I left the factory that night, Harrison shouted to me. I waited and he ran up to me. Did he want to use a knife on me? We smiled at each other.

"Did they ask you to fight me with gloves?" Harrison asked.

"Yes," I told him. "But I didn't promise."

"They want us to fight for five dollars each," he

said. "Man, if I had five dollars, I could make the first payment on a new suit."

"I don't want to," I said. "Why do a thing like that for white men?"

"To get five dollars."

I was watching Harrison and he was watching me. Did he really want to fight me for some reason of his own? He came up to me and I stepped away. "I need that money," he said.

"I don't," I said.

For another week the white men in both factories asked us to fight. Again Harrison called to me one evening as I was on my way home.

"Come on and fight," he said.

"I don't want to. Now they know that we know what they tried to do to us."

"So let's get the money. You can use five dollars, can't you?"

"Yes."

"Then let's fight for them."

"I would feel like a dog."

"To them both of us are dogs," he said. "Look, let's fool those white men. We won't hurt each other. We'll just *pretend to fight*, see?"

"All right," I said finally. "I'll fight."

The fight took place one Saturday afternoon. Each white man who came to see it dropped a *coin* in a hat on the floor. Only white men were allowed in. As the gloves were put on my hands, I looked at Harrison. What was going on in his head?

---

pretend to fight, act as if we were fighting
coin: see picture, page 93

We began, and at once I saw that I had not thought enough about the fight. I could not pretend to fight. I didn't know enough about boxing to do that, nor did Harrison.

The white men sat smoking and shouting dirty words at us.

"Hit him!"

"Oh, fight, you niggers!"

I struck at Harrison with my left, and he landed high on my head. Before I knew it, I had landed a hard right on Harrison's mouth, and blood came. Harrison shot a blow to my nose. The fight was on, was on against our will. I hit harder. The harder I fought, the harder Harrison fought. We felt anger at the white men who had made us do this. Then the anger crept into our blows, and blood ran into our eyes, half blinding us. We fought until we nearly fell with tiredness. Then the white men stopped the fight.

I could not look at Harrison. I hated him and I hated myself. I took the five dollars in my hand and ran home. Harrison and I did not speak to each other after that day. The white men tried to make us fight again, but we said no. I felt I had done something unclean, something which I could never forget.

10

There was a *library* near the river, but Negroes were not allowed to read the books. I had gone to the library several times to get books for white men on the job. Which of the men would help me to get books? I thought of one man after another. Finally I spoke to a man most of the white men did not like because he was an Irish Catholic.

"I want to ask you something," I whispered to him one day.

"What is it?"

"I want to read. I can't get books from the library. Will you let me use your card?"

"My card is full most of the time."

"I see," I said.

"What book do you want?"

"A book by *H L Mencken.*"

"Which one?"

"I don't know."

"Well, I'll think out something. But don't mention this to any other white men."

"I understand," I said. "I won't say a word."

A few days later he called me to him. "I've got a card in my wife's name; here's mine."

"Thank you, sir."

That afternoon I wrote a note to the library, asking for "books by H L Mencken" and signed the white man's name. I entered the library as I had always done when I had gone there to get books for white people. I

H L Mencken (1880-1956), important American journalist, writer of political and social works

At the library

stood and looked as unbookish as possible, waiting.

"What do you want, boy?"

I handed in the note.

"What books by Mencken does he want?"

"I don't know, ma'am."

"Who gave you this card?"

"Mr Falk," I said.

"Where is he?"

"He is at work. I've been in here for him before."

"I remember," the woman said. "But he never wrote notes like this before."

"You can phone him, ma'am," I said.

"You're not using these books, are you?"

"Oh, no, ma'am. I can't read."

I knew that I had won. I got the books and went out of the library. And that night in my room I began to read. Why did Mencken write like that? And how did one write like that? What was this ...? Yes, this man was fighting, fighting with words. Could words be used to fight with? Then maybe I could do the same thing. It was morning before I stopped. I went to work, but I kept thinking of what I had read.

I went to the library again and again. The first novel I read was Main Street by Sinclair Lewis. It made me see my boss in a different light. Now I felt closer to him. I felt now that I knew him and his narrow life, and this only because I had read a book about a man called George F Babbitt.

My reading made me feel that there was a great distance between myself and the world in which I lived. Every book that I read made me see and feel things in a different way. But I felt, too, that the white men around me knew that I was becoming different.

That winter, my mother and brother came to Memphis, and we got a place to live. I began to eat warm food, and to my surprise I found that I could read faster. My brother got a job, and we began to save money for the trip North. I told none of the white men about my plans. I felt that they would change towards me if I did.

Aunt Maggie came to see us in Memphis. We talked and talked about our plans. It was impossible for all four of us to go to Chicago at once; we did not have enough money. And if we waited until we had, we should never be able to go. We finally decided that Aunt Maggie and I would go first, though it was winter. Why wait until next week or month? If we were going, why not go at once?

When I told the boss, he turned round in his chair and gave me a long look.

"Chicago?" he repeated softly.

"Yes, sir."

"Boy, you won't like it up there," he said.

"Well, I have to go where my family is, sir."

"It's cold up there," he said.

"Yes, sir. They say it is," I said flatly.

"You think you'll do any better up there?"

"I don't know, sir."

"You seem to have been getting along all right down here," he said.

"Oh, yes, sir. But my mother is going. If she wasn't going, I would stay here and work," I lied.

"How are you going to act up there?"

"Just as I do down here, sir."

"Would you speak to a white girl up there?"

"Oh, no, sir. I'll act there just as I do here."

"Oh, no, you won't. You'll change. Niggers change when they go North."

I wanted to tell him that that was why I was going, but I did not.

I went to the post office for the last time. When I was back in the factory, I washed my hands, put on my hat and looked at the men who were working late. Mr Falk, to whom I had given back the library card, gave me a smile, and I walked to the *elevator* and rode down.

"You're lucky," said Shorty, the elevator boy.

I stepped out of the elevator into the street. I was half expecting somebody to call me back and tell me that it was a dream, that I was not leaving.

This was the culture from which I sprang. This was the fear from which I fled.

ELEVATOR

Questions

Chapter 1

1. How does Richard set fire to the curtains?
2. Where does he then go?
3. What happens to him afterwards?
4. Why does Richard kill the kitten?
5. Do you know anyone who has killed an animal? Explain.
6. What does his mother make him do in the evening? What do you think of that?
7. Why do they have no food in the house?
8. How many times does Richard start out for the store, and what happens?
9. Have you ever been afraid in the street? Explain.
10. How much money do the men in the saloon give Richard?
11. How does Richard learn to read?
12. And to count?
13. What does he learn from the other boys at school?
14. What happens to Richard's mother?
15. How much money does Granny give the family?
16. Why does Richard's mother send the two boys to an orphan home?

Chapter 2

1. Who is Ella, and what does she tell Richard?
2. What does Richard want to understand about whites and blacks?
3. Talk about Richard's parents and grandparents.
4. What happens to Uncle Hoskins?
5. How much money does Richard's mother earn in the doctor's house?
6. What happens when Richard is called to the blackboard?
7. Has anything like that ever happened to you?
8. In what year does this chapter end?

Chapter 3

1. What do the black boys talk about?
2. How much money does Richard earn at his jobs?
3. How much would you earn?
4. What happens to Richard's mother?
5. State two ways in which the uncles and aunts help the family.
6. Do people help each other like that where you live? Explain.
7. Where do the two brothers go?
8. If you were in Richard's position, would you sleep in that bed?

Chapter 4

1. Why do you think Aunt Addie wants to beat Richard?
2. Why didn't Richard tell Aunt Addie the name of the boy who threw walnuts on the floor?
3. What would you do if you were Richard in that kitchen?
4. What do you think about Richard's story of the Indian girl?

Chapter 5

1. Talk about Richard's first day at the new school.
2. What does Richard do when school is over?
3. Would you care if you had to go without food for twelve hours?
4. What does Richard do to make money?
5. If you sold newspapers, would you think about what was written in them?
6. What happens to Grandpa?
7. Why does Richard want to leave home?
8. How about acting out the scene between Richard and Granny?

Chapter 6

1. Where does Richard first get a job and what does he do there?

2. How much does he earn at his different jobs?
3. What does he do with his story?
4. How long do you think his story was?
5. What does Richard earn from his story?
6. What do his friends at school say? What does Granny say? What would you say?
7. Why does he dream of going North?
8. Do you have a dream of going somewhere? Explain.

Chapter 7

1. What summer jobs does Richard try?
2. Do you take a summer job? Explain.
3. Why do you think Richard does not want to take the speech written by the principal?
4. Why do you think the principal says that Richard may not pass?
5. What does Richard say about going to college? What do you think of that?
6. What does Richard do on the night of graduation?
7. Can you think of other ways in which people can be "bought"?

Chapter 8

1. Where does Richard find a job?
2. What do they do to the black woman?

3. Why do you think the white men in the car offer to help Richard?
4. Can you explain what then happens?
5. What is Richard's job at the movie house?
6. What plan does the man in the café tell Richard?
7. What two questions does Richard ask himself?
8. How much do you think the fifty dollars is worth to Richard?
9. Where does he want to go now, and why?

Chapter 9

1. Where is Richard when this chapter starts?
2. How would you find a room in a new town?
3. Where does Richard work?
4. What does Mr Olin say about the other black boy?
5. What does Richard say? What would you say?
6. Why do the white men want the two black boys to fight, according to Harrison and Richard?
7. What do **you** think is the reason?
8. Why does Harrison want to fight?
9. What would you do in Richard's place?
10. What is the fight like?
11. How does Richard feel after the fight?

Chapter 10

1. What does Richard do to borrow books at the library?
2. What effects does his reading have on him?
3. What events take place that winter?
4. What does Richard's boss think of his plan?
5. How far is it from Memphis to Chicago?
6. Now, how about reading this story in the original, as Richard Wright wrote it?